A WORD TO

"A" / "THE"

WISE WOMAN

MONICA T. ROSS

Dedication

*Dedicated to the Anointed and Wise Women who are
the Daughters and Warriors of the Most High GOD.*

Acknowledgment

To my ABBA, thank You for guiding me to
write this book on Your behalf.
I am truly grateful.

TABLE OF CONTENTS

Introduction

The difference between "A" Wise Woman and "The" Wise Woman is not too far apart. It is about how each allows GOD to teach them to be who they are and to be wise. "A" Wise Woman is one who comes into her understanding that GOD was always with her during her process, and these processes have made her wiser. "The" Wise Woman has completed her process and now stands in her purpose and destiny in GOD. She understands that process is what GOD uses to make her wiser, and it brings her deeper in HIM. Both women understand that being "A" Wise Woman and "The" Wise Woman is a process that only GOD HIMSELF can teach them.

A WORD TO

"A"

WISE WOMAN

"Love"

Love is patient and kind. It is not conceited, and it is not hateful. It does demonstrate its physical attribute of being a word of action. To love is not easy to step into because it requires action on behalf of the person who is required to give unto another for an act of wrong, the act of betrayal, or deceit. But no matter what act the person has done, the feeling of not wanting to love a person who has done these things to you will leave you in a pit of bondage. In this life, you do have a choice. A choice to learn to love or to continue to allow the person to have power over you, your feelings, emotions, mind, and most of all your heart. It is not easy, but once you understand that love will help conquer all those acts and even sooth your emotions, you will begin to experience a freedom that only you can give yourself.

Matthew 5:43-45 NKJV

"You have heard that it was said, You shall love your neighbor and hate your enemy.' But I say to you, love your enemies, bless those who curse you, do good to those who hate you, and pray for those who spitefully use you and persecute you, that you may be sons of your Father in heaven; for He makes His sun rise on the evil and on the good, and sends rain on the just and on the unjust."

"That Reflection"

The hardest thing to do is to look into the mirror and see the flaws that reflect below the surface. It is easy to cover up hurt, anger, fear, anxiety, worry, and other emotions with Maybelline, Cover Girl, Mac, Avon, Neutrogena, Rimmel or Lo'Real but they do not last forever. The hardest thing to do is to acknowledge that below the beautiful exterior is an interior that is lost and can't find or doesn't want to find the solution to help bring both the exterior and interior together to be one. But once you see it, acknowledge it, and then work at it so that you can be beautiful inside as you are outside.

Matthew 7:3-5 NKJV

"And why do you look at the speck in your brother's eye, but do not consider the plank in your own eye? Or how can you say to your brother, 'Let me remove the speck from your eye'; and look, a plank [is] in your own eye? Hypocrite! First remove the plank from your own eye, and then you will see clearly to remove the speck from your brother's eye."

"You are For-Given" A Conversation

"I just called. Nothing important just saying good morning to my lovely sister. How are you? I do hope all is well. All is well here. I went to the gym yesterday and I walked and ran the track...WHEW!!! This girl is really out of shape; but with God's help and me doing the work as we say, "They ain't ready." Hahahahaha!!!! So seriously, this is overdue. I have been talking about it, but with me finally facing what is going on with me, I am getting better and more able to love me for me. That is because my God loves me for me. He said to me that I have forgiven you; you need to forgive yourself. Especially for those things in my past I had no control over, especially from my childhood."

It is wonderful when God wants to help you but you have to do the work, and have the faith that really moves God to do the impossible where it seems impossible to you. To realize that God wants to take away the hurt, the disappointment, anger, rage, the broken heart, and turn it around for your good. Who wouldn't want to serve a God like Him?

Luke 7:47 NKJV

"Therefore I say to you, her sins, which [are] many, are forgiven, for she loved much. But to whom little is forgiven, [the same] loves little."

"Possess"

As we know the children of Israel had possessed the land. They are God's chosen people and were being suppressed by Pharaoh from Egypt. God uses His servant Moses to lead them out of Egypt and to guide them to the land promised to them. But due to their disobedience to God, about totally destroying the nations in the land, they are now being harassed by these nations. They began to worship the gods these nations served.God tested them to see if they will continue to serve Him through their trials. But their answer was "No." They don't serve Him, so God caused the other nations to continue to come up against them. This scripture is powerful, and it applies to us today. "...*So whatever the Lord our God takes possession of before us, we will possess.*" (Judges 11:24) In other words, you don't have to do a thing about what others have taken from you or what someone is trying to take from you; marriage, home, money, peace, joy, worship, praise, health, or family.

As long as you are obedient to God, and not be like the children of Israel and walk in disobedience you will be able to possess whatever and wherever God has taken possession for you. Some of these nations that came up against Israel wanted their land back, as demonstrated in Judges chapter eleven. But always remember, that after God has gone before us and taken possession of whatever belongs to us, all we have to do is go in and possess. GLORY TO GOD!!! Let God take it from them, for you to possess it.

Judges 11:24 NKJV

"Will you not possess whatever Chemosh your god gives you to possess?

So whatever the LORD our God takes possession of before us, we will

possess."

"Be New or Stay Old"
A Conversation with a Sister

Some things haunt me too. Like the hurt of being betrayed by family or friends. But I do not let it have power over me. It is part of my past, not part of my today or future. You are a new creature in Christ because of what He did. *"Behold old things are passed away, behold all things become new."* (2 Corinthians 5:17) It is up to you to be new....or stay old. Nothing is wrong with going to your therapists, but what you need is to understand is that God has provided a way for you. You have to have faith, but you have to do the work as well. If I can walk out of my hurt that had me crippled for a long time, you can begin to pull away from that which is holding you back. When you start to pull away, God is going to cut the rope. He is waiting for you to go forward. Go forward!

Yes, it will be scary but you need to know you are more than that which is holding you back. If He told me the answer for me to walk out of my hurt, then He will most surely show you what you need to do to be set free from that which has held you back. Be Free, Sister.

John 8:36 NKJV

"Therefore if the Son makes you free, you shall be free indeed."

"The Past Factor"
A Conversation with My Sister

I can take a lot from people, but when I've had enough, I will let you know. And that is what happened. I had reached my point of "enough.'" Besides, I've moved past all that and pressing forward. The reason or reasons some of us can't move forward is because we are too busy looking back. Even allowing people to speak to us about the past and causing us to look back. I'm moving on from all things in my past. I can't change it nor can I make it better if I could go back. So I'm pressing forward into what God has placed before me. It was time for me to grow up and stop having the pity parties and be the Woman of God He created me to be. I'm not allowing anyone to take me back to where I came from. The path is set before me and I choose to follow it and not turn around and go back. It is like a new adventure into the unknown with God, but knowing that He has laid the path for me to follow.

So, my lovely sister, I'm not concerned about my past or how I got to where I am now because of it. I will not consider what happened. I ask you to do me a favor, and I will return the favor. Let us press forward into the things and the promises of God and leave our past in the history pages of life. We can't change it, but one thing about a history lesson it will teach you what not to do in the present and the future. So I choose to learn from it but not go back to it. AMEN!!!

Philippians 3:13-14 NKJV

"Brethren, I do not count myself to have apprehended; but one thing

[I do], forgetting those things which are behind and reaching forward

to those things which are ahead, I press toward the goal for the prize

of the upward call of God in Christ Jesus."

"His Peace"

Today, as I was meditating on the word "peace," the Lord began to give me revelation about "His peace." I know the Lord will help you understand more in-depth about "His peace" as long as you will seek His face and ask Him. We have heard the saying, *"If God gave it to you; then no one can take it from you."* But when it comes to our peace of mind, peace of our emotions, and peace of our hearts, oftentimes we allow others to take the very peace that God gives to us.

Oftentimes we open ourselves up to those who appear to care, but actually they do not. We allow them into our world of peace and yet, somehow without warning and not being aware of it, they take some of our peace. Because as human beings it is important to us to have that human contact with others. Some of us love to help others in need, to uplift those who are downtrodden, love to listen and help any way we can, and then they stop talking to you, shun you, use you and even sometimes betray you.

It is very important to understand to hold on to the peace that God has given us, and allow that peace to wash over us when someone has trespassed into and onto our peace. To be honest, they have taken some of our peace away. Guard your peace as you would guard your heart and your mind. Don't let anyone disturb or take your peace. Only you can determine who comes into your world of peace and whether or not you will allow them to continue to take or steal your peace. Love ya'll and God Bless.

John 14:27 NKJV

"Peace I leave with you, My peace I give to you; not as the world gives do I give to you. Let not your heart be troubled, neither let it be afraid."

"Close Your Mouth"

We are to walk in our God given authority. Even when Paul had the thorn in his side, he complained to God about it. The only thing God told him was His grace was sufficient for him to accomplish what He had anointed him to do. So you have a thorn in your side where you work. If you are not on your guard, you can get caught up in gossip and other mess that is happening around you. Those things you see and hear that are not right are manifestations of the greed of man and his selfishness. God teaches us to be quick to listen and slow to speak. (James 1:19 NKJV) Some things we have to put into practice and strengthen ourselves in God and the anointing that is on our life.

I will be honest, God has closed my mouth many times and I would sit there wondering why I am not responding. Because the power of our words lies in what we speak forth. It is time for us as the

People of God to speak life. To speak the Word of God. The only way to do that is to have His Word continually be in our mouth; from sun up to sun down and even when we are sleeping. That is what Jesus did to the tempter, throughout His ministry, when He was on the cross, and that is what He does today sitting at the right hand of God still speaking the Word of God. We should be so saturated with the Word of God to the point that what comes out of us, is not the bread we eat but the very Word of God.

Proverbs 13:3 NKJV

"He who guards his mouth preserves his life, [But] he who opens wide his lips shall have destruction."

The Question: "What will separate you from the love of God?"

Will it be "Ole boy" in whom you know is not going to leave his wife? It doesn't have to be him. It could be another man. You hold on to him because no one else is paying you attention. So you cling to him until someone else comes along and turns your head. As women, that is what we do. We hold to the one that is giving us the attention we crave and yet they cannot give us their full attention. We will hold fast to them in the hopes they will make us their lady and hopefully, their wife.

Ohhhhhh...the many times I've done this and was left feeling like I gave too much of myself and didn't know how to get me back. I recommend to you that you begin to pay more attention to yourself than to these men who may be in your life for no good reason or just there for a season. Especially, if that joker is married. Girl, all kinds of warning signs should be going off when a married man comes into your picture frame. Girl, take your foot with your red bottoms on and kick his tail out of the picture. Stop giving him you and stop giving yourself to him. Love yourself more, hug yourself more, be kind to yourself more, understand yourself more, and be you more than ever. Be you and stand by your requirements of yourself. Do not change them unless it is to make you better than you were a second ago, a minute ago, an hour ago, a day ago, a week ago, a month ago, a year ago, and even years ago.

I love you, my lovely sister and will always keep you in prayer. I will be here for you whenever you need me. But begin to spend more time with God. Yes, even when He doesn't answer, know that He heard you and loves you dearly.

Romans 8:39 NKJV

"Nor height nor depth, nor any other created thing, shall be able to separate us from the love of God which is in Christ Jesus our Lord."

"A Shift in Friendship"
The Reality of When it is Done

On the days that followed, I even went into her office and thought we were past it, but her actions were showing and saying differently. She stopped coming into the office to speak. I even passed her in the hallway and we had a conversation and again I assumed we were past it, and again her actions showed differently. People choose sometimes to be in the place they are in. I've had others stop speaking to me, accused me of things I had no part in, and accused me of something I've done that had no direct impact on them. I'm not about to keep shifting and changing for people who don't want to shift or change how they are acting. It means I'm shifting and changing to suit them and not for God or myself. I'm not shifting or changing for foolishness or pettiness.

As friends, we are going to disagree on things. That alone should not cause a friendship to end. As the world continues to focus on what is said and done, it appears that some friends want you to conform to them and not them to you or for it to be an understanding of who both or all are to each other.

She has not known me long enough to know that I would not hurt her directly. I expressed to her as such, but she took what I said and tried to use that to her advantage about something that had absolutely nothing to do with her. Not one of us is the same and no we will not see eye to eye on everything which is why God made each of us different. If she chose to use this as a means to stop speaking to me, then let it be so. I've tried, but she stayed the way she was, and now, I'm leaving her there.

I'm keeping my focus on God, so I don't go back to where I used to be; focused on the fact I want to kick their behinds, cuss them out and even get even. Now which way should I go? I'm going in the direction that God has placed before me and leaving those things behind that have no real push nor encouragement for me. I have to continue to be transformed according to the Will of God in and on my life, and not conform back to the way I used to be.

Psalm 37:23 NKJV

"The steps of a [good] man are ordered by the LORD, And He

delights in his way."

"Flowers or Weeds"

Flowers are flowers and weeds are weeds. There are some weeds that look like flowers, but their main purpose is to choke the life from an actual flower and anything else around it. Some flowers are like vines that produce beautiful flowers, but there are also weeds that look like beautiful vines, but will wrap around whatever it is connected to, and will begin to overtake and choke the life from whatever it is wrapped around. Some of us have weeds in our life that need to be cut, unwrapped and uprooted. Then some of us have beautiful flowers and vines that are there to help us that we need and must keep. It's time for you to know the difference.

You will know the difference of the flowers and the vines who are there to encourage and push you forward to where you need to be in God. They see your beauty and see who you really are to Him, and will encourage you to get where He needs you to be. The fake flowers and vines will often question or even criticize your dreams and hopes in what God has created you to be; they won't encourage but instead discourage nor push you forward. They also see your beauty and see who you really are to God, but will do their best to stop you or hinder you.

Matthew 13:22-23 NKJV

"Now he who received seed among the thorns is he who hears the word, and the cares of this world and the deceitfulness of riches choke the word, and he becomes unfruitful. But he who received seed on the good ground is he who hears the word and understands it, who indeed bears fruit and produces: some a hundredfold, some sixty, some thirty."

"New"

Today is a new day. Do you not know this or have yesterday's disappointments, sorrows, mess, betrayals, and etcetera keep you in their oldness? Knowing that you cannot change what has happened, it happened, but at some point it gets old, so old that it now has cobwebs. But God has given us a new day and has done a new thing, made a road in our wilderness to walk on, and given us living water in our deserts. But we miss it because we are still focused on yesterdays. So let go of yesterdays that are already gone and focus on the new day that is today and give God the Glory for it.

Isaiah 43:19 NKJV

"Behold, I will do a new thing, Now it shall spring forth; Shall you not know it? I will even make a road in the wilderness and rivers in the desert."

A WORD TO

"THE"

WISE WOMAN

"Apology"

Only apologize for that in which you are wrong for. It helps to clear the conscience and removes unnecessary weight. But don't be moved from the stance of what is right and true about you. Love yourself first and everything about yourself. There is nothing like a confident woman who understands who she is and where she is going. And if a man can't understand or handle it, then he isn't the one. If a friend is constantly degrading or speaking negatively of your dreams or your hopes, well, sometimes it is best not to tell them. Or you may have to weigh the relationship and determine if they are an encourager or a discourager. You make the choice. Don't let anyone, be it a man or a woman, bring you down to their level. Keep rising to your destination because only you can get yourself there.

Job 42:1-6 NKJV

"Then Job answered the LORD and said: I know that You can do everything, And that no purpose of Yours can be withheld from You. You asked, 'Who is this who hides counsel without knowledge?' Therefore I have uttered what I did not understand, Things too wonderful for me, which I did not know. Listen, please, and let me speak; You said, 'I will question you, and you shall answer Me.' "I have heard of You by the hearing of the ear, But now my eye sees You. Therefore I abhor myself, And repent in dust and ashes."

"Real Love from A Man"

The word love is so loosely used these days by some men, because they know that it is what we want to hear. We believe it even though the actions of the man are completely opposite. But to be honest, it has to be felt and not when it comes to sex. Sex will make you say anything under its influence, because sex is a drug...LOL!! "This is your mind on sex....snap, crackle, pop and sometimes boom!"

Love is special between two people who understand one another. It's not used to tear one down or for one to tear down the other. That is not love. As women, when a man loves us, we should feel secure in their love; not having to defend who we are or argue about something that is important to us. And most of all they should love us for where we came from and understand what it took to get us there. To love us to the next level by holding us up and encouraging us to push on.

At this point, if they are not doing that, well, you might want to tell them and even show them that "rock kicking" is still in effect. If you need some rocks, I'm sure there are some rocks out there who won't mind you borrowing a few of them to give to him. In fact, I got the hook up with some of them. Just let me know. LOL

1 Corinthians 7:1-5 NKJV

"Now concerning the things of which you wrote to me: It is good for a man not to touch a woman. Nevertheless, because of sexual immorality, let each man have his own wife, and let each woman have her own husband. Let the husband render to his wife the affection due her, and likewise also the wife to her husband. The wife does not have authority over her own body, but the husband does. And likewise the husband does not have authority over his own body, but the wife does. Do not deprive one another except with consent for a time, that you may give yourselves to fasting and prayer; and come together again so that Satan does not tempt you because of your lack of self-control."

"Familiar"

We become so familiar with ourselves, family, and even people we befriend. But have we become familiar with God? I was reflecting on things that had become familiar to me when dealing with men. I see their actions that are familiar; what they are saying, how they present themselves as being interested but not really, they need their ego boosted, they take more than they give. It's all familiar. And yet in knowing all this familiarity of men, why do we as women, continue to deal with the familiarity? Not only in men but in women as well.

Not saying it is a bad thing, but there comes a time when you have to stop falling into familiarity. Be free from it, and move forward into your destiny in God. It's essential to become more familiar with God and, even more, familiar with whom God has created you to be. I expound on this because as we draw near to God, He begins to help us notice the familiarity of ourselves when it comes to people we let into our circle. Especially the subjectivity of "familiarity" of the actions of people that cause us to travel down memory road and revisit the past. After all, it is boring, unproductive, and not to mention it is one-sided. Sometimes, we are the reason we get stuck in these familiar places.

The wonderful revelation about God is that He changes not, but He does help us to change. Some of the changes involve familiarity of ourselves and people who come into our lives. If you are becoming a "new" creature in God then why do you continue with familiarity? The kind of familiarity that brings disappointment, heartbreak, disbelief, mistrust, lack of confidence, staleness, and stagnation. It is not productive nor does it push you to change or shift to where God is leading you.

The beauty of this is that once you recognize the familiarity (as I have done), you can now begin to remove yourself from it. What do I mean? When you recognize that it is familiar to you and how it makes you feel or where it leads you, you now have the option to remove yourself from it. GLORY TO GOD for revelation!

For me it means backing away and even backing down, and not

allowing my emotions to overpower my thinking the situation through. My past actions, when it came to men, were so familiar that I'm so glad that I can now recognize the familiarity of it, put a stop to it before it leads to disappointment, put walls up, and walk in discretion. You just don't know how happy I am that I now can do this and feel good about it. It has taken a long time for me to get here and I am not going back!

Oh, one other thing. If you don't get it under control or remove it from you, then you will begin to go back to your familiar behavior. For me, I built what I called safety walls to try and counteract the familiarity. I would put on my tough girl skin, and make sure my demeanor showed the "Don't mess with me, or I will come for you" attitude. However, I did not realize it was causing some men not to approach. I did it because I knew or thought they were not about anything.

Well baby, not anymore. Let them strong, mighty, and anointed Men of God come this way…the walls of Jericho are coming down.

Psalm 41:9 NKJV

"Even my own familiar friend in whom I trusted, Who ate

my bread, Has lifted up his heel

against me."

"A Word of Promise"

Good Morning Lovely Daughter of God,

As I was reading the Word of God last night, you know sometimes that particular scripture will rise up from the pages and greet you with confirmation, help settle your spirit, or ease your heart and mind. I've been reading the Book of Joshua. As you may know, Moses has died and now Joshua, the son of Nun, has the charge. And boy does he charge in and possess the land that God has promised. I wonder how many of us are charging to possess what belongs to us...just a question for thought.

For you, in whom God has made a promise, to hold fast to what He has said, for He alone will bring it to past. In other words, it won't be you, your husband, your children, immediate family, girlfriends, bosses, or even the dust mites that may be in the corner of the room that manifest your promises. It will be God who brings it to pass and because He is God it will come true. So if you are in your valley, keep moving, or climbing to reach the top of the mountain. Keep climbing!

Remember only you and God can get you there. Be blessed and love

ya!

Joshua 21:45 NKJV

"Not a word failed of any good thing which the LORD had spoken to the house of Israel. All came to pass."

∾

"Separation, with Replacement"

When God began to separate me from certain people, at first I didn't understand what was going on. It bothered me a lot because I enjoyed being around these folks. Then gradually the separation came, nothing that I had done but nevertheless a separation had started. I wasn't naïve to what was happening. But in time, I soon realized that it was God that was doing it. I didn't ask Him why I just went with it when it happened.

Afterwards I began to hear things that were going on with them. Not real bad things but things I didn't need to be around. I was glad that God had created the separation. With time, He replaced them with others who shared the same faith as me. I understood that an unsaved man or woman would not have the same understanding of the things of God. Therefore, I knew that I needed to be around like minded people. He allowed me to understand that it didn't mean I would not go hang out with them or be around them. I understood

52

what they did I could not be a part of because God was now requiring me to be separate and to be holy. It was not an easy task when it seems as though they were having fun and I was at home looking at television.

I made the decision to serve Him. He didn't force me. I chose to worship and praise God. And with my obedience to Him, He has transformed me into the Woman I am now. A process that was not easy but the results are wonderful.

Numbers 6:8 NKJV

"All the days of his separation he shall be holy to the LORD."

"OUT OF THE PIT"

I'm finally out of my pit as demonstrated yesterday. Girl, God swept through the church yesterday. Now, I am just waiting to see what He will do with me next... AMEN!!! There is nothing like being free and victorious over what had held me bound. Even people who have known me for this long of time, have noticed I don't go off like I used to. I am at peace with myself and love me more than I ever did because God showed me that He loved me and was willing to help me get through the jungle I was tangled in.

I don't wear a mask anymore. I don't look at other women and wish I could have their hair, lashes, body shape, ecertra. That was a false pretense of who I really am. I am the Daughter of the Most High God, a Father God, who loves me dearly and unconditionally.

2 Corinthians 6:18 NKJV

"I will be a father to you, and you shall be my sons and daughters says the Lord Almighty."

"Godly Husband Material?"

Listen, my beautiful sister. When a man speaks openly in public about your status with him then believe it. When it comes to you and him, a true sign that a man is really interested in you is that he will do most of the chasing; and even confirm your status publicly when it comes to you. He that "...findeth a wife..." (Proverbs 18:22) And I mean he will chase. You have to be careful that the table is not turned and you are the one doing the chasing. You have to use the wisdom that God has given you and use it wisely to protect you.

Yes, we expect the men of God to be just that; a man of God, and they are. Yet you must remember that they are men who also wrestle with who they are and how God is dealing with them. You, as a woman, must know when to release so much to a man, but not so much that you can't pull back. Knowing these boundaries is very important. Nothing hurts more when you have given so much of yourself to a man, and he has taken and not given the same in return, whether he is saved or not. Understand that no man gets to play with the Daughters of God, whether they are saved or not. However, we have to be careful to ensure that we do not get played with, which is why you ask Father and use your wisdom when a man comes into your life.

Know when to pull back, but still maintain the relationship of a friend. Being a friend is priceless because despite it all, you still have unlimited access to their life. Because of the friendship, a man is willing to share more about himself than he would with someone else who is just above the surface friend. That means he will come to you and share, when he won't with others. You have the kind of access that some women wished they had, and that is far more important than trying to rush it into something more than friends. Friendship is a solid foundation. I've learned to listen and pull back when necessary, and even though it bothers me to do so, I must protect myself at all costs. I've come too far to allow myself to return to the state of mind and heart I was once in.

God has demonstrated that He will and is faithful to complete what is started. As the wise woman, I stand on His promises to me.

Do the same and all the things that you, as the wise woman, desire,

need, and even want will come to pass but only through God.

Continue to allow God to bring you to where He is taking you. With

your obedience to Him, there is nothing He won't withhold from you.

The promises of God reach far into our generational future.

2 Corinthians 1:20 NKJV

"For all the promises of God in Him [are] Yes, and in Him Amen, to

the glory of God through us."

"Decisions"

Hey Lady,

Thanks for your guidance, heartfelt love, and concern. Love you for it. I will admit that when we, as the People of God, do not uphold our Father in the esteem He desires or see things that should not be in church (I know we are not perfect), it does bother me. Even I don't always do what He requires of me to do at times, and He has to correct me for my errors and ways. But as I am being changed, I understand it is better to listen to God than lean to my own understanding.

Sometimes you have to step back, look, and reflect at what you are doing. And learn not to be so wrapped up in what others are or are not doing. If you need a moment from being around the people of God, it is okay. Jesus even went away to be alone.

From time to time, things we see in church will cause us to be distracted and vexed in our spirit, but it is God who deals with us individually and corporately as a church. The tests, trials, and tribulations will come for each of us but it is entirely up to us, as individuals, if we submit under the hand of God or continue to travel our own path or route. It is that now my awareness of who He is to me has been heightened.

To do what is pleasing to God is important to me. I can't allow others in the church or whomever is in my life change what He has done. I am trying to explain to you that I allowed people to push me into a pit by their very words or actions towards me. God has helped me climb out and I'm not going back because of people. And that includes those in the leadership status in the church.

We, the people, are the church in which the Holy Spirit resides in. Going to a physical building is where we go to be taught a new word, get more understanding, and allow God to move through the church to touch us where we are. But what has been revealed is now the church is more of a hang out for those who come to see what others are wearing, find out the latest gossip of what member has done what, where spectators gather, and participation is few. It has become a place of controlling people by invading into their lives instead of just preaching the word. If the people need spiritual counseling, then allow those who need it to come.

The Word of God says, "...if I am lifted up from the earth, will draw all men unto me." (John 12:32) Let us focus on lifting Him up so the people can see Him and not us. I just feel in my spirit, as I told a friend, there is so much more than what is before our eyes, and if it means that I have to separate from some people in my life (who God is telling me to let go) then I will do it.

As I said before, it is about Him and not about us. The path that is set before us is for us to travel. There will be some who will be with you all the way, some will drop along the way, others will turn away, some will betray you, and others will envy you and will try to stop you. But the one thing that remains true you are the one traveling the path. It is up to you to decide to continue and run your race set before you.

Deuteronomy 30:15-16 NKJV

"See, I have set before you today life and good, death and evil, in that I command you today to love the LORD your God, to walk in His ways, and to keep His commandments, His statutes, and His judgments, that you may live and multiply; and the LORD your God will bless you in the land which you go to possess."

"Out of My Pit"

Sorry for this long email. I know you are just getting to know me and I am getting to know you. I know that God will reveal some things about me to you as He will with you to me, but He does not reveal all. My life history is one of hurt, anger, mistrust, betrayal, disappointment, heartbreak, mental abuse, and physical abuse. So, you can only imagine what was imprinted into me. None of which I wish to return to, nor will I allow myself to ever return to. I won't allow anyone to control me but God Himself.

So, if I hear it or see it coming from other people I will remove myself from their presence and pray for them. I am brand new out the pit and I won't let anyone pull me back into it. And I do mean no one. It has always been up to us whom we allow into our lives. If you can't uplift me to my destination in God, nic-pic with me, and try to bring me down to your level, after all the processes I've been through to get where I am now, I will most definitely separate myself from you and love you from the distance. AMEN!!

Psalm 40:2 NKJV

"He also brought me up out of a horrible pit, Out of the miry clay, And set my feet upon a rock, And established my steps."

"Come"
A Conversation with My Godly Sisters

Good Morning Daughters of God,

This has been in my spirit since Sunday, and is still moving me today. To back this up with scripture Matthew 14:29 says, "And He said, Come. And when Peter came down out of the ship, he walked on the water, to go to Jesus." What is funny about this is that the Disciples were away from shore. I could tell you the story but in order for faith to arise in you go read Matthew 14 to know how Peter came to walk on the water. At this moment, launch into the deep with God.

For many of us, we tend to stay in the shallow pool where it is safe because it only comes up to our ankles and we can see what is at the bottom. Right? Right. I raise my hand to this. So, we will stay right there and never move into the deep water, because either you can't swim, like me, don't want to mess up your new hairdo, like me or is the other reason fear like me? Because in the deep you cannot see the bottom and it means the water will be up to your neck. That is the same way with God. He doesn't mind us being in the shallow end, but sometimes when it is time He needs for us to move into the deep with Him. You have to make the choice to follow His voice, read His Word, and trust Him when He says, "Come."

There are times we miss the voice of God when He speaks to us. One because we don't know His voice when He speaks. Two we are so busy listening to others who tell us how to move from the shallow into the deep of our lives. Most of these folks can't even begin to get into the shallow of their own lives. Three we simply don't want to listen and miss what He is telling us: which is why it is very important to listen when God speaks.

Some of you will ask, "How do I know the voice of God?" His voice will direct you into and onto the right path. But in order to hear Him you have to have a relationship with Him and wait for Him to speak. Even if He doesn't say a word, wait until He does.

How do you do this, launch deep with God? This is the a way of starting to launch into the deep with God. It means to read your Bible and meditate on the Word and pray. Prayer is a communications line from you to God's ear. What we misunderstand about prayer is the formality of prayer. This stops many of us. There is no set way to talk to God. Just be you. Understand He is God. Go boldly to Him but humble before Him. I speak to Him daily and on a regular basis because He helps me through the day. For me, it is where I can really let God know how I feel. It is just like I talk to people, the real deal of how I feel. I don't hold back from Him. Trust He already knows and He is waiting on you to say it.

Finally, go to church with other Disciples of Christ that share in the same faith and understanding of God. I've learned there is nothing like the Woman of God in whom God has allowed me to come into my life. When I need to vent I can go to these women and say whatever is on my mind. Not everyone can take me. But the women, in who I've confided in, have proven themselves to be trustworthy and we have developed powerful relationships that I cherish. And to be honest, I don't confined in everyone. You have to be careful in placing "you" into others' hands. A lesson I've learned real quick. So go get ready to launch into the deep with God, because

He won't leave you to go deep alone.

Matthew 14:27-29 NKJV

"But immediately Jesus spoke to them, saying, 'Be of good cheer! It is I; do not be afraid.' And Peter answered Him and said, 'Lord, if it is You, command me to come to You on the water.' So He said, 'Come.' And when Peter had come down out of the boat, he walked on the water to go to Jesus."

∞

"Old You Vs. New You"

Never let anyone know how they affect you. I say this because I'm going through this and it is not easy when the old you battles with the new you. It leaves me tired, unsure, afraid, scared, not knowing, and uncertain. It also has me having thoughts of if it is right, leave it, walk away, let it go, drop it, run from it, hide from it, stay away from it, ignore it, shut it out, or completely remove it. This is what my old self does to my new self and it is hard. It pushes me into tears and almost stops me from moving forward. I always hated the roller coaster ride, but it is no one's fault but mine when I get on it and ride not knowing when I can stop it.

It comes from my past relationships with guys. One minute I can be up and the next I'm down. A continuous cycle of up and down, up and down, up and down, up and down, and me not having the knowledge or enough sense to get off. Or do I want to? I want to get off. I have protected myself from men this way for so long. But I'm learning the only way to move past this is to just dive completely off the coaster. Fall knowing that God will catch me or not let me hit the ground. I get up, brush off the dirt, and walk like I have arrived. I'm going to do that as of this day.

I'm diving off the roller coaster and walking on steady ground. It is long overdue that I get a grip on myself and allow the new me to come forth and force the old me into the back where she belongs. As she stays back there, in time, she will completely fade away. So this Woman of God is going to love and love hard. And no matter what it sounds like or looks like I will look past it and see the good in it. If it doesn't help me grow or move me into my next level then it has to be left on the path.

Ephesians 4:22-24 NKJV

"…that you put off, concerning your former conduct, the old man which grows corrupt according to the deceitful lusts, and be renewed in the spirit of your mind, and that you put on the new man which was created according to God, in true righteousness and holiness."

"Got to Grab It"

Question: Do you "get" a hold or have you "grabbed" a hold of God?   If you "got" a hold, how strong is your hold to Him. If you "grabbed" a hold of Him, how much of Him do you have, a little or a lot? Just some questions for you to ponder around with. Here is an appetizer to help. The word get means to gain possession of; to seek out and obtain; to receive as a return. It's past and past participle of get. The definition of grab is to take or seize by or as if by a sudden motion or grasp; to take hastily; to seize the attention of.

If you put the meanings of these words together and mix God in it would look like this… To succeed I have to gain possession of and continuously seek out my God given assignment. This is necessary in order to obtain and receive the experience of God by doing all I can to make an impression on Him by an action of a sudden motion or grasp hastily to obey Him that will seize His attention. The choice is easy. So use both words "got" to "grab" a hold of God!!! I just love when the Holy Spirit does this....Amen!!

Deuteronomy 10:20 NKJV

"You shall fear the LORD your God; you shall serve Him, and to Him you shall hold fast, and take oaths in His name."

$$\infty$$

"Who Is Talking To You?"

Good Morning Lovelies,

Just want to share this with you as it really hit me last night. Oftentimes, the enemy will come and speak into your ear to do something that may seem right to do, but in reality it is not. When you are in your valley or climbing the mountain, he will come and try to deflect or deter you from reaching your destination. What I am saying is that if what you do in response to what the voice has spoken to you and it causes you further disappointment or grief then you know it is not from God. The Word of God brings life, joy, and fulfillment and not the opposite.

One day, I went on Facebook. I don't do it often, but that voice spoke and said go check their Facebook page and you will see the real deal. I didn't pause to wonder why I would do that, because I thought it was God showing me something I needed to know. I looked at Facebook and was disappointed and bothered by what I read on someone's page. It wasn't anything real bad, it just bothered and saddened me. Then a revelation hit me. God isn't messy when He is dealing with us. He will simply tell us upfront when we are ready to hear it or when it is necessary to push us and tell us even when we don't want to hear It. He does this to get us to our destiny not to deter us from getting there. He doesn't do things from a sneaky spy point of view to cause you to go searching for those things that are not like Him. I really mean this revelation hit me not long after I looked on Facebook. Honestly, I should have been in the "Book" instead of looking for something not worth on Facebook. Amen!!!

I just want to encourage you that when that voice speaks, stop, and discern to whom it is really coming from. Does it bring forth rightness and truthfulness in its tone or does it bring sneakiness and cunningness to have you do something not worth it? It wasn't worth me going on Facebook and looking for something that was going to cause me to be saddened and disappointed. Pay attention to this especially when you are in the middle of your process.

I'm so glad God can reveal that foolishness. I don't know about you all, but I don't like being made or being made a fool of. So this morning as I sang my way into work, with God, I reminded the enemy

who I was.

John 10:5 NKJV

"Yet they will by no means follow a stranger, but will flee from him, for they do not know the voice of strangers."

"Perfect, Establish, Strengthen, and Settle" (PESS)

Good Morning Women of God and Daughters of the Most High,

I was reading the Word this morning, and you know a certain scripture will come out strong. I have been reading 1 Peter and my favorite verse from this book is verse nine. Read it. But this morning in the final chapter this word stood out to me.

1 Peter 5:10-11 NKJV

"But may the God of all grace, who called us to His eternal glory by Christ Jesus, after you have suffered a while, perfect, establish, strengthen, and settle you. To Him be the glory and the dominion forever and ever. Amen."

What caught my attention was "after you have suffered a while." We all know we do not want to suffer through anything. Whether it is an emotion, issue, problem, our relationships, and even to ourselves by doing right with our earthly bodies as well as our spiritual bodies. But looking at this word that says "after you have suffered a while." That means we will suffer through something but how we handle it determines if we will be in the words that follow "perfect, establish, strengthen and settle." But the question is, "Are you willing to go after being perfect, established, strengthened and settled" while you are suffering?

Yes, I know I am sending this long email, but this is getting me to an honest question from God. The Word of God says "...faith without works is dead." (James 2:17) In order to obtain and surpass the suffering by your faith, you have to push to achieve perfect, establish, strengthen and be settled by allowing God to place you on the Potter's wheel. You will still have the cracks of your suffering but now you are being perfected, established, strengthened and settled according to His Perfect Will.

God told me this a long time ago, as I was taking a Physical Training (PT) test (which I knew I was going to fail because I did not prepare for it after having my son) if you put forth the effort I will do the rest. Of course, I failed the PT test as I knew I would, but I began to prepare for the next PT test by doing the push-ups, sit-ups, and running. Needless to say, when I took it again I passed. What am I saying? I "suffered" from not passing my PT test the first time, but with "perfect" preparation, "establishing" myself to pass, "strengthen" myself by doing what was required on my own time, I was able to "settle" the right score on my PT test...AMEN!!

"A House Built"

Psalms 127:1 is clear except if the Lord builds it, you labor in vain (paraphrased) Consider this question. How is your home at this moment? Is the Lord over it or are you laboring in vain to keep it? Do you ask the Lord for guidance concerning your home or do you run with your own blueprint with the lines not drawn straight? Do you cry out to the Lord concerning the city you live in, or do you just watch what happens daily on the news of another crisis that is in the city? Trust me ya'll, I'm getting this too. Ouch!!! Let us continue to pray, and cry to the Lord concerning our families and the cities we live in. Amen!!! Prayer does change things. You only need to put it to use. Amen!!! God bless.

Psalm 127:1 NKJV

"Unless the LORD builds the house, They labor in vain who build it;

Unless the LORD guards the city, The watchman stays awake in

vain."

"It Is Nothing New"

The Lord has been dealing with me about this and bringing back to my remembrance all the times both men and women have either hurt, betrayed, stabbed me in the back, broke my heart, talked about me, ridiculed me, called me names, left me, used me and my heart, used my mind and body, my giving, and the list goes on and on. I am talking about me, but you can place yourself in this because we all have experienced this. The Word of God says it is nothing new. (Ecclesiastes 1:9) If this is so, then why does it become a surprise to me when different people, who are now new in my life, do the exact same thing that people before them have done. It should not be new to me because it has been done before.

So, now what do I do when the same thing keeps happening but it is now a different person who is doing it? I will keep it real. My first impulse is to do a Rambo on them by reverting back to my military skills and use them for what I was trained to do. But seriously the

Bible says be too "…quick to listen," and "slow to speak" as well as slow to anger. (James 1:19)

Well, let's do this. Recognize it and don't react to it. Just recognize the "nothing new" and move on. Yes, it does hurt when the new person or someone you've known all your life does the same thing. The point is, it is "nothing new" you haven't experienced before. Now that you know there is "nothing new under the sun," what are you going to do about the new people and even the older ones who are in your life, who are doing the same thing to you that you have dealt with from your past? Below is a recommended list on what to do when people in your life do the "nothing new."

1. Recognize it.
2. Grieve about it, but only if you need too; each of us is different.
3. Pray about it. Fervent prayers of the righteous prevailed much. (James 5:16)
4. Let God fight for you.
5. Move on.

Ecclesiastes 1:9 NKJV

"That which has been is what will be, That which is done is what will be done, And there is nothing new under the sun."

"Fasting and Prayer"

Remember what Jesus said "these things come through fasting and prayer." (Matthew 17:21) Other scriptures talk about prayer, but the Lord had me notice this one about fasting and prayer. Before Jesus began His ministry, He fasted for 40 days in the wilderness. After He had fasted, then the tempter came. The adversary never comes for you when you are at your full strength but when you are weak. He comes in those areas of your life that you have not let God show you that needs to be dealt with or He has shown you and you just miss what He was revealing.

If you noticed, the truth behind fasting was that Jesus was more alert than He was hungry. The adversary thought that because he was hungry he was more vulnerable. But the truth was that Jesus was more strong from the fasting than if he was full of food. It is because He brought his flesh under subjection to His spirit. Have you not noticed that when you are fasting you are more strong in the spirit than the flesh?

You are where you are to fast and pray for those in close range to you and for the people who are in bondage of the enemy; we all are. Allow the anointing on your life to shine forth in the darkness around you. Even a pin-head of light will shine in the darkness lighting the way for others to follow out of darkness and into the illuminating light of God. Heaven suffers violence and the violent take it by force. (Matthew 11:12) Take control of the atmosphere around you and push back the darkness. The anointing on you is strong. Use what God has given you and that is to be that light in darkness, no matter what you hear or see, nor what they do. And yes, I could choke some of them some folks who mess with me but God has been good to me even in this fasting He has been good.

Matthew 17:20-21 NKJV

"So Jesus said to them, 'Because of your unbelief; for assuredly, I say to you, if you have faith as a mustard seed, you will say to this mountain, Move from here to there, and it will move; and nothing will be impossible for you. However, this kind does not go out except by prayer and fasting.' "

∿

"Who Dropped You?" Move Forward

Who dropped you? My prayer for you is for you to push past and move forward in your life. Allow God to be God in your life. Yes, there are some things you will have to let go of in order for God to give you what He has designed and ordained for your life. God has a place for you.

Oftentimes, we place the wrong things into our hands and we allow it to control our life to a certain degree. You have to make a decision that will bring you peace, while at the same time it is hurtful because you know in your heart of heart that it is not good for you. The tough decision of let someone go has to be made. I've done it and it hurt like hell. Yes, sometimes it haunts me but in the end I had the peace I needed. If my peace is disturbed then there is a problem.

It really hurts when someone you care about stops talking to you suddenly and with no reason, but you have to accept that they showed you who they were even though sometimes we saw it from the very beginning. Many times, God will protect us and sometimes we don't even realize that it is He who is protecting us. Instead of looking at it like a blessing, we look at it as a mistake we made and now we are left feeling we should have been more careful or should not have waited for so long before we finally realize they were just who they were. Now we have given so much of ourselves to them that we don't know how to get it back. God has you as the apple of His eye. You are His daughter and His Woman of God.

Psalm 17:8 NKJV

"Keep me as the apple of Your eye; Hide me under the

shadow of Your wings."

"Watch What You Say"

As the Wise Woman and the Daughter of the Most High God, remember when operating in prophesy it is to bring "...edification, exhortation and comfort." (1 Corinthians 14:3) There is correction when it pertains to prophesy, but this is exercised from the office of a Prophet. This is the one who has been recognized and revealed by God Himself that He has called a person into that office. The Bible gives us an example when Nathan, the Prophet, corrects David for his affair with Bathsheba. (2 Samuel 12)

Only move when God tells you to move and not because you know something or sense something about a person. Remember you are accountable for what you say to people. Be very sure when God speaks. If you have not mastered knowing when He is speaking, seek Him and ask Him to know His voice and His voice alone when He speaks. One thing about God is that He is about uplifting, restoring, healing, and chastising the ones He loves. He will give you what you ask for in order to operate in your gift He has given you. He doesn't leave us hanging.

God desires for us to operate in prophesy from His standpoint and not ours. Remember this is God's anointing and prophesy is mainly speaking the Word of God. If you are not speaking what God says, then you are in error. If what you are saying to the person does not bring them peace, joy, or comfort then you are in error. If rebuke is mandated, then be sure it is God speaking and not yourself from your perception because you know about it. If you do, you are now operating in your flesh and not from your spirit and are pretty much prophe-lying. You have gone to them and used what you know carnally instead of going into it spiritually; using God as a means to do it when He has not sent you nor told you anything

Joel 2:28 NKJV & Act 2:17 NKJV

"And it shall come to pass afterward That I will pour out My Spirit on all flesh; Your sons and your daughters shall prophesy, Your old men shall dream dreams, Your young men shall see visions."

2 Peter 1:21 NKJV

"...for prophecy never came by the will of man, but holy men of God spoke [as they were] moved by the Holy Spirit."

"Microwave or Baked Patience"

James 1:3-4 says "...testing of your faith produces patience. But let patience have its perfect work in you..." So, when your faith is tested you have to let patience work perfectly in you. You have to build your patience when your faith is tested. It is no different when you work out to build your muscles. The world we live in is so microwaveable. We think we need something to happen within few seconds or a few minutes that we forget that sometimes it is best to put some things in the oven and let it bake to perfection. So, let patience bake inside you that when your faith is tested your patience is baked to perfection......AMEN!!!

James 1:3-5 NKJV

"…knowing that the testing of your faith produces patience. But let patience have its perfect work, that you may be perfect and complete, lacking nothing. If any of you lacks wisdom, let him ask of God, who gives to all liberally and without reproach, and it will be given to him."

"Accountability"

Listen, some of us don't want or feel we need someone to help us in our walk with God. But God tells us to encourage one another. But encouragement comes with accountability and many of us don't want that. We want the words of encouragement but not the words of accountability. We are taught that when someone loves you they will tell you the truth. Well, encouragement and accountability are part of "truth." You have to have both. They actually help balance you in your walk with God. Don't cheat yourself, from those who are willing to do this because they really do love you.

1 Thessalonians 5:11-13 NKJV

"Therefore comfort each other and edify one another, just as you also are doing. And we urge you, brethren, to recognize those who labor among you, and are over you in the Lord and admonish you, and to esteem them very highly in love for their work's sake. Be at peace among yourselves."

"Not Funny"

You know what "is not" funny. That we are the People of God and yet we won't' pray for each other. We won't fellowship with other churches. We won't encourage each other. We have allowed what is not of God into His House. We have accepted what the world says we are not. We battle for attention with our Pastors. We let the spirits of competitiveness, control, jealousy, strife, discord, separation, division, witchcraft, ill-speaking, gossip, mess, drama, procrastination, and the like run rapid in the House of God and even in our own lives and homes. We won't come to church to get a Word from God to help us in our daily lives. We use the excuse that all churches are messy, the Pastor only wants our money, but we won't ask God where to go where His Word is taught by Pastors after His Heart. We do not conform to the Word after we have heard it in order for it to heal and deliver us. We turn a blind eye to sin and condone what is not like God. We will speak what the world says, but won't even utter a Word of God…"It is not funny."

Round 2 of "It is not Funny." The consequences of the seeds you sow come to greet you. And you wonder why your life is upside down and twisted this way and that. Stop trying to blame the enemy all the time. Those seeds you planted a long time ago, your own harvest has come in. Guess what, you are still planting those same seeds. Are you ready for the same harvest…again? "It is not funny."

James 1:22-25 NKJV

"But be doers of the word, and not hearers only, deceiving yourselves. For if anyone is a hearer of the word and not a doer, he is like a man observing his natural face in a mirror; for he observes himself, goes away, and immediately forgets what kind of man he was. But he who looks into the perfect law of liberty and continues [in it], and is not a forgetful hearer but a doer of the work, this one will be blessed in what he does."

"Do You Prophesy, Woman of God?"

Have you prophesied over your life today Woman of God? Have you spoken the Word of God over that situation, problem, issue, or trouble? God has given you the ability to prophesy over yourself, your family, your health, that situation, and anything else going on in your life. The reason why sometimes you don't prophesy over yourself is that you have more of what the world has placed into your mouth than replacing it and having the Word of God placed there. Begin to use that Spiritual Listerine, The Word of God, to rinse your mouth clean by speaking it. Then use The Word of God to prophesy over your life. Also, stop listening to what others have to say about your life. The more you listen, the more it will soon come out of your mouth.

Act 2:17-18 NKJV

"And it shall come to pass in the last days, says God, That I will pour out of My Spirit on all flesh; Your sons and your daughters shall prophesy, Your young men shall see visions, Your old men shall dream dreams. And on My menservants and on My maidservants I will pour out My Spirit in those days, And they shall prophesy."

Notes

Merriam-Webster.com (2020). "get" Retrieved from

https://www.merriam-webster.com/dictionary/

get

Merriam-Webster.com (2020). "Grab" Retrieved from

https://www.merriam-webster.com/dictionary/grab

www.ingramcontent.com/pod-product-compliance
Lightning Source LLC
Chambersburg PA
CBHW071536150726
48000CB00002B/823